Dreaming Your Reality

Seeing God's Vision Come to Life

BRETT AIKEN

authorHOUSE®

AuthorHouse™
1663 Liberty Drive
Bloomington, IN 47403
www.authorhouse.com
Phone: 1-800-839-8640

First published by AuthorHouse 12/20/2010

ISBN: 978-1-4520-2346-5 (e)
ISBN: 978-1-4520-2350-2 (sc)

Library of Congress Control Number: 2010907223

*Printed in the United States of America
Bloomington, Indiana*

This book is printed on acid-free paper.

About The Author

Brett Aiken was born on August 13, 1983. As a senior in high school, Brett was born again. After his senior year, he answered the call to preach the Gospel at seventeen years of age. Brett obtained a Christian Studies degree from North Greenville University and a Masters in Christian Leadership from Liberty Theological Seminary. Brett and his wife Erica have been married since August of 2006. Brett's greatest passion in life is sharing God's message.

DEDICATION

This book is dedicated to Faith Fellowship Church in Pendleton, South Carolina.

"It was noised that Jesus was in the house." Mark 2:1

TABLE OF CONTENTS

Chapter 1

DREAMERS ADD AN "H" TO IMPOSSIBLE

The world will try to wake you up from your dreams by giving you sleepless nights. Don't let negative people discourage you from doing great things. Since the beginning of human civilization, true leaders have pushed through negativity and hatred to accomplish their dreams.

> "Then Joseph had a dream, and when he told it to his brothers, they hated him even more." Genesis 37:5

Have you ever noticed that most people are like Joseph's brothers; THEY HATE DREAMERS. The world we live in will do whatever it can to extinguish the fire in your heart. The truth of the matter is that we need more people like Joseph who can dream the dreams of God. Dreamers and visionaries bring life where there is extinction; water where there is drought; vitality where there is despair. My prayer is that God would raise up some dreamers!

Dreamers and visionaries bring life where there is extinction; water where there is drought; vitality where there is despair.

Do you know why the average person's life is a nightmare? They have stopped dreaming. Do you know why the average church is a nightmare? The pastor has stopped dreaming.

> *"Where there is no vision, the people are unrestrained."* Proverbs 29:18

No matter who you are or what field of life you are in, you need a fresh and exciting vision of what God wants to do in your life; you need a dream! Christians should be the most alive, exciting, and dynamic people in a town. If that is the case, why does the average church resemble an insomnia clinic rather than a dream factory? We are in desperate need for God's people to start dreaming again. One person with a dream is equal to a force of ninety-nine who have only an interest.

Someone said after Walt Disney World was created that it was too bad Walt Disney didn't live to see what was built, but in reality, he did see it...that's why it's here. Everything that seems common to us today was at one time impossible; from riding on a train to flying in a plane. A few decades ago, making a call on a cell phone would seem impossible. Now, almost every person in the United States has one!

Everything amazing started as a dream. A dream is the ability to see into the horizon and then, from the end result, work in the present to accomplish the goal that is in the future. Isn't that what God is doing even now? From the beginning, God has been working from the end result: He desires for a group of people to spend eternity worshipping Him because they receive forgiveness of sin and the salvation that He offers. He has been working to accomplish His vision since the beginning of time. Before the world began, He mapped out the destination. Someone once said that the wise man knows the destination before he buys the ticket. Get a dream, and then pursue it with all your heart.

How does God's dream for our life become a reality? You must first understand that dreamers always add an "H" to impossible. When you add an "H" to impossible it becomes "Him-possible." Hallelujah, I don't care what it is, with God it is possible!

> *"For nothing will be impossible with God."*
> Luke 1:37

> *"The things that are impossible with people are possible with God."* Luke 18:27

You need to get out of your heart that some things are impossible; a dreamer takes the impossible and adds an "H" and it becomes HIM-POSSIBLE. All things are possible for Him. One thing I never want to hear in our church is "that's impossible" or "we just can't do it." We can do it because we can add an "H" to impossible.

When you really think about it, what is impossible? Even the laws of our world like gravity, matter, and death don't apply to God. Peter could walk on water because of the power of God. Jesus walked through a wall because of the power of God. Lazarus came back from the dead because of the power of God. My point is that we limit our own dreams because we use a word called impossible when we should realize that nothing is impossible for God.

Dreamers realize that you can take the impossible and add an "H" to it and it becomes Him-possible; God will make that dream in your life possible. More often than not, we let the idea that our dream is impossible steal our passion. Don't let anybody steal what God has already given you. The Bible teaches that the Devil is a thief, and he will do anything he can to steal away the dream that God has given you. Jesus did not come to steal but to give us an abundant life.

Don't let anybody steal what God has already given you.

The first key to dreaming your reality is to always add an "H" to impossible. Many people have a dream and then at the first sign of resistance they give up. For many, the first person to tell them it is impossible causes that dream to go by the wayside. Change your mindset about what is possible and what is impossible. Never underestimate the power of our Father.

I remember as a young boy we had a huge field beside our house where we would play baseball. At the far end of the field there was a gray wooden fence that had more splinters than nails. Although none of us had the power to hit it there, the fence served as the outfield wall. It was inconceivable to think that anyone could hit the ball over that old wooden fence. Since we did not possess the power to hit it that far we just assumed it could not be done; we considered it impossible. One day my dad stepped off the lawnmower and walked toward us as we were playing. He motioned for us to throw him a pitch at home plate. He boasted of how he was going to hit it over the old wooden fence on the other side of the field. We could not believe he said such a foolish thing! It was impossible to hit it over that old fence. After a few pitches, we saw something we had never seen before; the impossible was now possible. I underestimated the power of my father.

We thought something was impossible because we had never seen it done and because we did not possess the power to do it. Just because we did not have the power to do it did not mean that my father did not have the power to do it. Never assume something is impossible just because you have never seen it done. Something may be impossible for you, but that does not mean it is impossible for our Heavenly Father.

The first step to dreaming your reality is to add an "H" to impossible. If God has put a dream in your heart you can believe that with Him it is possible. God wants you to be able to see your dream come to life.

Chapter 2

GET YOUR FEET WET

When you think about seeing your dream become a reality, I am sure that you have some obstacle that you must get through for your dream to come to life. In fact, if you don't have any obstacles I would say you don't have any dreams. Part of seeing your dream become a reality is conquering something that tries to defeat you.

In the Bible, the book of Joshua describes the events of a group of people who were more than conquerors. God wanted these people to cross to the other side of the Jordan River and establish themselves as a nation. For years there were many obstacles that kept them from doing so. Finally, they stood at the Jordan River with their goal in sight. As the people stood and gazed at the river, they faced their biggest obstacle yet; the

Jordan River was at flood stage. The river was flooding and it seemed impossible to be able to cross it. This was one of those moments where it must have seemed they were taking two steps forward and three steps back.

The children of Israel had come so far. They had been through so many trials and so many hardships. I am sure many questions began to flood their minds… how can we get across without drowning…what are the children going to do…what about the Ark of the Covenant? If these people would have been a church of the 21st century they would have formed a committee, looked at their options, and then decided that nothing could be done and headed back to Egypt! Lucky for them they had a leader who had a dream in his heart from God.

Joshua knew that for this dream to become a reality the people were going to have to demonstrate faith. Joshua looked the people in the eye and encouraged them to believe God to move the waters! He told the priests to step out into the water and believe God for the rest.

> *"It shall come about when the soles of the feet of the priests who carry the ark of the Lord, the Lord of all the earth, rest in the waters of the Jordan, the waters of the Jordan will be cut off, and the waters which are flowing down from above will stand in one heap."*
> Joshua 3:13

In essence, Joshua told the people to get their feet wet. He knew that if the people would put their dream into the hands of God that God would not let their dream go under. God can keep a dream from drowning. Joshua knew that God was greater than any obstacle in their path.

It was not a coincidence that God brought them to cross the river when the river was at its roughest. God wanted them to face a problem they could not handle. Sometimes God wants us to face problems that we cannot handle because He wants to show us that He can handle them. Whether it is high water or just a high water bill, God is greater than our problems.

The prophet Isaiah said,

> *"When you pass through the waters, I will be with you; and through the rivers, they will not overflow you. When you walk through the fire, you will not be scorched, nor will the flame burn you."* Isaiah 43:2

God can keep a dream from drowning

Throughout the entire Bible, we can see that God is greater than any problem we may face. God is greater than any problem in life! Joseph realized that God was greater than an Egyptian prison. Daniel realized that

9

God was greater than lions. Jonah realized that God was greater than his own disobedience.

Have you realized that God is greater than your own sin?

What is your problem today? I promise that God is greater. Your problem is not an obstacle to your dream...it is an opportunity to see God. Before God would fix their problem in the book of Joshua they had to step out there into it. I heard someone say that God was attracted to weakness. God loves when we make ourselves vulnerable to Him. God loves when we step out into a venture that we cannot do on our own. God loves faith; God loves when we get our feet wet.

- Getting your feet wet may mean walking an aisle
- Getting your feet wet may mean standing up for what is right
- Getting your feet wet may mean getting baptized
- Getting your feet wet may mean going on a mission trip
- Getting your feet wet may mean giving God more than 10%

You will never see God move until your feet are wet. I remember as a seventeen year old boy when God called me to preach. The thought of being a preacher had never even crossed my mind. The last thing anyone would have ever thought Brett Aiken would become was a preacher! God saved me on New Year's Eve during my senior year of High School. Over the next few months my life changed in amazing ways. By the time I graduated, I had such a hunger for the word of God that I was sharing it with every person I came in contact with. I remember the day that God called me to preach the gospel. I did not have any idea what I was going to do or where I was going to go, but I got down beside my bed and by faith told the Lord that I was His. At that moment, I had so much faith that God would take care of every detail from there. On that day I got my feet wet. When we demonstrate faith is when we get our feet wet.

> *"And without faith it is impossible to please Him, for he who comes to God must believe that He is and that He is a rewarder of those who seek Him."* Hebrews 11:6

Your dream will stay a dream until you are willing to trust God and get your feet wet. God is waiting to do a miracle in your life but until your feet are wet it will not happen. In the book of Joshua, as soon as they got their feet wet the river divided and allowed the people to pass through. I like how it says that the people stood on dry ground. God can dry up your problem until you are able to pass through it!

- The presence of God can dry up your cancer

- The presence of God can dry up that leak in your finances
- The presence of God can dry up that loneliness
- The presence of God can dry up that low self esteem
- The presence of God can dry up the ocean that is your sin

Whatever obstacle you face today that is keeping you from achieving your dream is no obstacle for the presence of God.

God can dry up your problem until you are able to pass through it

---

If you want to dream your reality, then you must get your feet wet.

Chapter 3

If You Can't See, Then Listen

There will come a time in the life of your dream that you will temporarily lose the vision of what God wants to do. It is possible that as you read this book there is something standing in your path of vision that makes Jesus look blurry. The devil will do everything he can to try to keep you from seeing God clearly. I don't care what the devil puts in front of you; God can get to where you are.

One of the devil's biggest lies is that our problem denies us access to Jesus. I know that God can get to where we are because He already came to where we are when He left Heaven and came to this earth! It doesn't matter what is going on in your life today, God can get to you. If you can't see Him, then listen for Him. If you can't listen for Him, then reach out and touch Him. If you can't touch Him, then call out to Him. If you can't call out to Him, then crawl to Him. Do whatever it takes to get to where He is. No matter the blockade, God has made a way.

There is a man in the Bible by the name of Bartimaeus. Bartimaeus was a blind man in need of a touch from God. His story is found in Mark 10:46-48. *"Then they came to Jericho. And as He was leaving Jericho with His disciples and a large crowd, a blind beggar named Bartimaeus, the son of Temaeus, was sitting by the road. When HE HEARD that it was Jesus the Nazarene, he began to cry out and say, Jesus, Son of David, have mercy on me! Many were sternly telling him to be quiet, but he kept crying out all the more, Son of David, have mercy on me!"*

Blind Bartimaeus could not see Jesus so he listened for Him instead. The moment he heard that it was Jesus passing by he cried out to Him. Isn't it interesting that the Bible says many people were sternly telling him to be quiet? The world doesn't like it when we cry out to Jesus. When you make up your mind to leave your situation to get to where Jesus is, the world will criticize you.

If you can't see Him, then listen for Him. If you can't listen for Him, then reach out and touch Him. If you can't touch Him, then call out to Him. If you can't call out to Him, then crawl to Him.

I don't know about you, but I have made up my mind about Jesus. I'm not going to be quiet. I'm not going to shut up. I'm not going to stop telling people that Jesus is the answer to all their problems. Criticize me if you want to, but I am going to go where Jesus is.

You cannot let criticism keep you from going where God wants you to go. You cannot let criticism keep you from accomplishing your dream. Bartimaeus didn't care about the world's criticism because he knew Jesus was the one that could make his dream a reality.

After Bartimaeus cried out to Jesus, Jesus took notice. *"And Jesus stopped and said, call him here. So they called the blind man, saying to him, take courage, stand up! He is calling for you."* Mark 10:49

The Bible says in verse 49 that Jesus stopped when Bartimaeus cried out to Him. I'm so glad that we serve a God that will stop for us! I'm glad that He didn't pass me by that night I asked Him to save me. I'm glad He listens to me every time I have a burden. I'm glad that He takes the time to make dreams a reality.

The Bibles tells us that after Bartimaeus called out to Jesus that Jesus called out to Bartimaeus. When God calls out to you, miracles can happen. When God calls your name, burdens are lifted. When God calls your name, vision is restored. When God calls your name, sins are forgiven. When God calls your name, things can change.

Jesus told him to be of good cheer and rise up. When the world knocks you down, you need God to call you to rise again. Maybe you have been knocked off your feet today. Maybe your dream has been blurred. You don't need a psychiatrist or a financial broker or more medicine; you need Jesus Christ to say take courage and stand up!

- When Jesus says take courage you don't have to fear
- When Jesus says stand up you don't have to fall
- When Jesus says open your eyes you don't have to squint

Quit squinting at your dream and open your eyes up and see what God can do. The story ends with Bartimaeus receiving his sight. Something that started as a dream ended in reality when Bartimaeus truly turned it over to Jesus. Have you really turned it over to Jesus today? Bartimaeus could not see but he could listen and he heard the voice of God.

When God calls out to you, miracles can happen. When God calls your name, burdens are lifted. When God calls your name, vision is restored. When God calls your name, sins are forgiven. When God calls your name, things can change.

I don't know what the obstacle is that's keeping you from seeing your dream become a reality. The good news is that God can get to where you are. Don't believe the devil's lie that you can't have access to God's presence. Through the shed blood of Jesus Christ we can have access to God's presence! God will make a way for your dream to become a reality. Whatever the case, if you can't see, then listen.

Chapter 4

HE CAN KEEP WHAT'S OUT OF YOUR REACH

By this point you should have figured out that your dream is bigger than you. What I mean by that is you are not big enough to make your dream come to pass. There are many "self help" books on the market today: this is not one of them. The reason this is not a self help book is because I know what the Bible says, and it says we cannot help our self. We are in trouble because of something called sin, and we cannot do anything about it on our own; we need God.

God is the only one that can reach into our life and make it worth while. Our value comes from the fact that we are made in His image. One reason murder and abortion are wrong is because we are made in the image of God. It is no surprise that we live in a day where abortion is legal. Since the beginning of time, anytime

God is on the verge of shaking the earth, the devil puts it into the hearts of leaders to kill babies. Think about it. Right now, the Lord is awaiting His return to this earth. The devil knows that Jesus is close to returning for His church, and so the devil promotes the murder of innocent little babies.

When God was ready to send Jesus into the world the first time, the devil put it into the heart of King Herod to murder all the baby boys in the district. Even before that, Moses was born during the time in Egypt where all boys were slaughtered. Every time God is up to something big, the devil puts it in the hearts of leaders to kill children.

When Moses was born, the people of God were in desperate need for somebody to spark a dream of freedom in their hearts. God's people were living as slaves in the land of Egypt. I am sure the mother of Moses shared in this dream. She knew the law of the land which said that all little boys were supposed to be killed, but she had a dream in her heart that said something else.

The mother of Moses made up her mind that she was going to put her dream into the hands of God because she knew there was no other way that it would survive. She knew that she did not have the reach to protect her dream and make her dream grow into a reality. What did she know? She knew that God could keep what was out of her reach.

> "*Now a man from the house of Levi went and married a daughter of Levi. The woman conceived and bore a son* (Moses); *and when she saw that he was beautiful, she hid him for three months. But when she could hide him no longer, she got a wicker basket and covered it over with tar and pitch. Then she put the child into it and set it among the reeds by the bank of the Nile.*" Exodus 2:1-3

Every mother believes their child is special, but this mother recognized something different about her child. She could tell that God had a special plan for the life of her little baby boy. The Bible says that she got a wicker basket and commissioned him into the navy because she set him sailing down the river. By faith she believed that God would somehow preserve the life of her dream.

Is someone trying to murder your dream today? I have news for you. He can keep what's out of your reach. God is able to preserve your dream until it is His time to make it grow. It may not be the time for your dream to grow into maturity yet, but rest assured, He can keep what's out of your reach.

Some things are meant to be survived instead of conquered. That does not make for the best sermons, but it is true. Some things in life are meant to be endured.

Endurance is a word that we need to begin to focus on in church today.

Some things are meant to be survived instead of conquered.

You may be in a place in your life today where God wants your dream to survive. I promise you that He can keep what's out of your reach. It took eighty years for Moses to flourish into the leader and deliverer that we know him as today. Before he could flourish, he needed to survive.

The most interesting thing about the story of Moses is the word the Bible uses for "wicker basket." The same Hebrew word used for "wicker basket" in Exodus was used for Noah's "ark" in Genesis. Why is that important? Remember Noah and his family were in danger of being destroyed under the judgment of God, but God said if they would get into the ark they would be preserved. The ark was the protection of God whereby they would not drown with the heathens when the flood waters came.

God did the same thing for Moses that He did for Noah; God used an ark to preserve his life! God used an ark to keep him from falling into the hands of the enemy! God used an ark to keep him from drowning! (I hope you can see where I am going with this)

The ark in the book of Genesis and the ark in the book of Exodus represent the same thing; Jesus Christ is our ark! Jesus Christ serves as our safety. Jesus Christ serves as our protection. Jesus Christ keeps us from falling into the hands of our enemy. Jesus Christ keeps us from drowning when the waters get high. You need to understand today that Jesus Christ can take what is out of your reach and preserve it for you until it is time: He can keep what's out of your reach.

The Lord can keep your finances afloat. The Lord can keep peace in your home. The Lord can keep the enemy from getting his hands on your loved ones. The Lord can take the enemies hands off your loved ones. He can keep what's out of your reach.

You need to turn everything in your life over to God today. He can take something that is out of your reach and present it right there to you. Isn't that what He did with salvation? God took something we could never obtain on our own and made it possible for us to receive it. If you are not saved today, will you prayer this prayer to God right now.

Dear God, I know that I am a sinner. I believe that Jesus Christ died on a cross for me. Forgive me of all my sins and come into my heart and save my soul. I turn away from my sin and receive Jesus into my life. Help me to live for you the rest of my life.

Jesus has the power to forgive our sin and save our soul. He can keep what's out of your reach. You need to take all your hopes, dreams, nightmares and fears and place them in the ark of God to set sail down His path.

> *"And we know that God causes all things to work together for good to those who love God, to those who are called according to His purpose."* Romans 8:28

Put your job in that wicker basket and push it down His river today. Put your future in that wicker basket and push it down His river today. Put your children in that wicker basket and push it down His river today. Put your soul in that wicker basket and push it down His river today. He can keep what's out of your reach.

Chapter 5

HEAVENLY HONEY FROM THE
CARCASS OF OUR PROBLEM

Every problem is an opportunity to prove God's power. Every day we encounter golden opportunities disguised as insurmountable problems. When a problem comes our way, we need to learn to shake it off and use it to step up and be better for God.

I heard a story about a farmer who had a mule that fell into a well. The farmer thought it would be too much trouble to get the mule out of the well. Since the well was no good with a mule in it, the farmer decided to bury the mule in the well. All the animal rights people just had a heart attack. The farmer started gathering shovels full of dirt and dropping the dirt in the bottom of the well. As the farmer started shoveling dirt on the mules back he realized the mule started to shake the dirt off and then take a step up from the dirt under his feet. Every time a shovel of dirt hit the mules back he would shake it off and take a step up! Before long the mule stepped out over the wall of the well. The very thing that was supposed to bury him is what turned out to be the greatest blessing of all!

Many times in the life of a believer, the greatest obstacles are intended to be the greatest blessings. I love the story of Samson from Judges chapter 14. *"Then Samson went down to Timnah with his father and mother, and came as far as the vineyards of Timnah; and behold, a young lion came roaring toward him. And the Spirit of the Lord came upon him mightily, so that he tore him as one tears a kid though he had nothing in his hand…when he returned later to take her, he turned aside to look at the carcass of the lion; and behold, a swarm of bees and honey were in the body of the lion. So he scraped the honey into his hands and went on, eating as he went."* Judges 14:5-9

The story begins with *an attack.* One day as Samson was walking down his path, he was attacked by a lion. That is a pretty big obstacle! I have had some dogs attack me but never a lion. Maybe you have had a bad morning (flat tire, cold water in the shower, etc…but I doubt you have ever had a lion attack you). Samson's day started with a lion attacking him. You have probably never been attacked by a lion, but we can all relate to Samson in that we have been attacked in some way or another.

- Maybe you feel attacked by a person in your community who seeks to ruin your reputation.
- Maybe you feel attacked by some kind of disease.
- Maybe you feel attacked by some kind of bad news.

Everybody knows what it is like to be attacked in some way or another. Everybody has problems. The truth is that everybody has suffered at some point in their life. Life can be very hard at times. The question is-HOW DO WE HANDLE OUR PROBLEMS?

One of my favorite stories in the Bible is the story of Joseph. Later in the book I will give an entire chapter to his story. One of my favorite things about his life is that he used his problems to become his pedestal for success. Joseph had such a confidence in God that it did not matter what life threw at him. Joseph knew that God was in control and would use the good and the bad to accomplish something great.

> *"And we know that God causes all things to work together for good to those who love God, to those who are called according to His purpose."* Romans 8:28

Both Joseph and Samson understood that every attack was a possibility for blessings in the future. Let me ask you, do you realize that the attack on your life today may be an opportunity for God to do something great? Do not give up just because someone or something is attacking you. The key is to wait for the anointing of God to show up. That is the second thing I want you to see. We have already seen *an attack*. Now I want you to see *an anointing*.

The Bible makes a point to mention that the Spirit of God came over Samson so that he could defeat this lion that was attacking him. An anointing from God is greater than any obstacle that could come your way. Anointing means that God empowers you through His Spirit to accomplish a specific task.

An anointing is the touch of God on your life so that your problem can become your pedestal. You need to be anointed! An anointing is not just for preachers of the gospel or evangelists but for every Christian that is really hungry for the Lord. When you are anointed, you have the power to accomplish everything God wants you to.

The devil is terrified by God's anointing on our lives. The devil knows that if we get anointed we can change the atmosphere around us! Anointed prayers can change the world. Anointed hands can heal the sick. Anointed words can bring healing to the weary. We need to get anointed.

"I can do all things through Him (Christ) who strengthens me." Philippians 4:13

"That He would grant you, according to the riches of His glory, to be strengthened with power through His Spirit in the inner man." Ephesians 3:16

"O God, You are awesome from Your sanctuary. The God of Israel Himself gives strength and power to His people. Blessed be God!" Psalm 68:35

God wants to give you strength to overcome whatever the opposition is in your life. God can help you stop smoking; God can help you stop cheating; God can help you stop drinking; God can help you stop lying. The only way to truly see your dream become a reality is to get anointed and let God do it through you! God has the power to help us in any circumstance.

"And what is the surpassing greatness of His power toward us who believe." Ephesians 1:19

God has the power and it is available to us. Many Christians do not realize the amazing power that is available to us who believe; the problem for many is they do not believe. Without faith it is impossible to please God. If you do not exercise faith, it is like there is a loose cable between you and God.

I remember when I was in High School. I had a gold colored Ford Explorer that I loved. One day it went dead in the rain (all the Chevy people said "no wonder…it was a Ford). I stood in the rain for almost an hour trying to get that car started. I assumed I had a dead battery. I thought the problem was that my power source had lost its power. Finally, I realized that the battery was fine, but I had a cable that came unloose. As soon as I connected the cable back to the source, my car had all the power it needed. The problem was not the power source, but the problem was that I had a loose cable.

Faith is kind of like that cable. We have an infinite supply of power available to us, but if we do not believe we will never know anything about it. We will live our life standing in the rain complaining about a dead religion when we could be tapping into the power of God. Many people give up on God because they lose the faith. Instead of losing your faith, learn how to plug into the power and anointing of God.

When you have an attack on your life learn how to use the anointing of God to overcome it. That problem may be the very thing that God wants to bless you with. The story of Samson ends by Samson returning to the carcass of that lion. When he returns, he finds that dead lion filled with honey. (Some make a point to mention that this broke Samson's Nazarite vow but I think the application is still true) Samson saw his old problem be the very same thing providing him with something sweet-fresh honey. I believe the honey represents the blessings and goodness of God.

- The very thing that seemed out to kill Samson, the lion, became the source for God to bless Samson with.

I believe that is what God is telling you today...I want to bring some honey from your bad situation. God can bring heavenly honey from the carcass of your problem! Do not ever think that just because your dreams are being attacked that God is through with you. Most likely, He will use that attack to bring blessings to your dream. Your problem will become the pedestal for your dream. Remember, you must trust God by faith that He will bring something sweet from your problem.

Chapter 6

GOD CAN WALK ON WHATEVER YOU ARE SINKING IN

"Immediately Jesus made His disciples get into the boat and go ahead of Him to the other side to Bethsaida, while He Himself was sending the crowd away. After bidding them farewell, He left for the mountain to pray. When it was evening, the boat was in the middle of the sea, and He was alone on the land. Seeing them straining at the oars, for the wind was against them, at about the fourth watch of the night, He came to them, walking on the sea; and He intended to pass by them. But when they saw Him walking on the sea, they supposed that it was a ghost, and cried out; for they all saw Him and were terrified. But immediately He spoke

> *with them and said to them, Take courage;*
> *it is I, do not be afraid."* Mark 6:45-50

The disciples had just completed a very successful mission of healing the sick and preaching the gospel. They had shared in the miraculous feeding of five thousand people. It was then that Jesus sent His disciples away into a boat.

So it was after a time of miraculous ministry that Jesus led them into a storm. Have you ever felt like you were in a storm in your life? Have you ever felt like the waves of this world were beating against you and the salty water from being mistreated was burning your wounds? Have you ever felt like the boat that is your life felt like it was going under?

Maybe not. Maybe your life is all roses and cupcakes. Maybe you do wake up in the morning and you have a bird that sits at your window and sings a song to you. If you do, then I want a bb gun to shoot it because I have difficulties! I have problems. That is why I need a savior who can reach out to me when I am in trouble. That is why I need a savior who can reassure me when I am doubting. That is why I need a savior who will rescue me when I am sinking.

- I am like the disciples-without Jesus I am going under
- I am like Peter when he said I have no where else to go

- I am like Paul because God knocked me off my high horse
- I am like Zaccheus because I must have Jesus stay at my house
- I am like the woman caught in adultery because He took my accusers away
- I am like the thief on the cross because I am hung without Him

I don't know about you...but my life is not roses and cupcakes-I NEED A SAVIOR.

There is only one person that can right the ship if you are sinking. There is only one person that can take a drowning dream and make it float. There is only one person that can walk on what you are sinking in. His name is Jesus.

I love what the Bible said in verse 48 of that text... the Bible tells us that Jesus can see what is straining you. It is interesting because earlier in the text it said that Jesus went to a high mountain to pray. So Jesus was elevated high in a cliff of a mountain when He looked down and saw His disciples straining in their present situation. Now Brett Aiken cannot see clearly from a long distance away. When I drive I am spotting raccoons for mail boxes! But the good news is that just because I cannot see clearly from a long distance does not mean that Jesus cannot see you from a long distance.

> There is only one person that can right the ship
> if you are sinking. There is only one person that
> can take a drowning dream and make it float.
> There is only one person that can walk on what
> you are sinking in. His name is Jesus.

Rest assured today that even if your spouse cannot see what is straining you, even if your co-workers cannot see what is straining you, even if your pastor cannot see what is straining you-Jesus can see.

Your dream should be a strain. If it was easy then everybody would be doing it. It does not matter what is causing your dream to be a strain, Jesus is greater. Distance made no difference to Jesus. He did not even have to be in a place to speak a word for somebody because distance made no difference to Him. Demons made no difference to Him. He could make any demon begin to shutter because demons made no difference to Him. Disease made no difference to Him. It did not matter how sick a person was if He wanted to-they could be healed because disease made no difference to Him. Death made no difference to Him. He raised Lazarus from the dead and He ultimately was raised from the dead because death made no difference to Him. Disaster made no difference to Him. He could step into any complication and make it a crown for His glory because disaster made no difference to Him.

You see, we are not talking about a regular guy...we are talking about Jesus.

He knows your dream, and He sees what is straining you concerning your dream. The Bible says that once He saw them He didn't just stand there doing nothing, but instead, He came walking on the same thing that was sinking them! You see, He not only sees what is straining you, but also, He stands on what is sinking you.

Aren't you glad that Jesus can walk on what is sinking you?

Praise God that all things are under the feet of Jesus! Praise God that there is nothing that can attack you that He hadn't already defeated! Praise God that the God of the Bible walks on top of every single threat to us! He can walk on top of every single accusation. He can walk on top of every single sin. He can walk on top of every single demon. Jesus Christ took His sandals off after He died on the cross and put on some boots because He was going to show His authority and walk over every enemy.

> *"You have put all things in subjection under His feet. For in subjecting all things to Him, He left nothing that is not subject to Him. But now we do not yet see all things subjected to Him."* Hebrews 2:8

The Bible says that we do not see everything that is under His feet, but rest assured that everything is under His feet.

- No matter what it is trying to take you under, it is under His feet
- No matter what it is that has you down today, it is under His feet
- No matter what it is that is causing you to worry, it is under His feet

What you need to realize today is that He can walk on whatever you are sinking in. Your dream may be sinking, but He can walk on it. Your marriage may be sinking, but He can walk on it. Your finances may be sinking, but He can walk on it. The truth is that because of Jesus you can walk on it too. Remember Peter started walking on the same thing that was sinking them until He looked up and saw the storm around him.

God has given us authority to stand on everything that Jesus stands on.

> *"Behold, I have given you authority to tread on serpents and scorpions, and over all the power of the enemy, and nothing will injure you."* Luke 10:19

It is time for God's people to put some boots on and start stomping some things! No matter what it is today,

Jesus sees what is straining you and stands on what is sinking you. He also speaks to what is scaring you.

In the last part of the story Jesus speaks out to His disciples and takes their fear away. They were scared because they didn't know what was happening. Most of the time, that is what makes us fear too. We are afraid of the unknown.

Some of you reading this book are afraid because you do not know what tomorrow may be like. Some of you reading this book are afraid because you do not know where you will spend eternity. Some of you reading this book are afraid because you do not know what direction to turn next. Some of you reading this book are afraid because you have a child that is not doing the right thing. Some of you reading this book are watching as your dream sinks.

Do you know what you need? You need Jesus to speak to your situation. You need Jesus to speak to what is scaring you. He told His disciples to be of good cheer. That literally means to get happy. Why don't you take this moment to stop and ask God to help you "get happy" about what is scaring you. If you will get positioned so that God will speak to your situation, then your dream will not sink because He can walk on whatever is sinking you.

So often today we allow everything to sink us. We let the things of the world sink us spiritually. We let the things of the enemy sink us emotionally. We let stress at work sink us even when we come home. God didn't call us to sink!

Do you remember the old game where you try to sink your opponents battleship? Believe me, we have an enemy trying to sink the battleship of our faith. It does not matter what it looks like around you today, keep faith that God will keep your dream afloat; He can walk on whatever is sinking you.

Chapter 7

When All Your Hope Dies

There will come a time in your life, if not already, when what you hoped for seems to die. There will come a time in your life, if not already, when what you believed in seems unbelievable. There will come a time in your life, if not already, when what you trusted in seems untrustable. I am talking about when all your hope dies.

The Bible tells of such a story. In Luke chapter 8 we read about a man named Jairus. Jairus had a daughter at the point of death. He had hopes that Jesus could help him. He searched for Jesus and told Him about the situation. Jairus explained the urgency needed in the situation because his daughter was so close to dying. As they walked the direction toward the home where the little girl was, people began to press against Jesus making it very difficult to get to where they needed to go. It makes me think of rush hour traffic...you know how frustrating that can be...even for a preacher traffic can bring out the worst in you!

To make matters worse for Jairus, somebody comes up and touches Jesus and by doing so makes Him stop what He is doing and enter into conversation. Jairus must have been thinking that the clock was ticking and this hold up would cost his daughter's life. Sure enough, after Jesus helps this other person with her problem the news arrives that Jairus' little girl was dead.

What do you do when all your hope dies?

For Jairus, it must have seemed like all his hope just died. The Bible says that this little girl was twelve years old; for twelve years Jairus watched his dream grow up. For twelve years Jairus spent time with his dream. For twelve years Jairus nurtured his dream. For twelve years Jairus loved his dream, and now it was dead.

I do not know what it is like to lose a child. I am sure that someone reading this book knows what that is like. It is understood that burying your own child is the worst thing a parent could ever go through here on the earth. Everybody handles things differently and everybody grieves differently. The saddest thing is that some people lose trust in God when something so tragic happens. The saddest thing is that some people doubt that God is who He says He is just because they witness their dream die.

Listen carefully, just because it may SEEM LIKE God is letting your dream die does not mean that He is not bringing life to somebody else's dream at the same time. Our present situation should never make us doubt that God is who He says He is. Mark it down, if your dream looks dead, there is somebody, somewhere, whose dream just came back to life.

In that story I just told you, the reason Jesus stopped was because He was bringing life to somebody else's dream. You will not believe this, but the Bible says that the woman that Jesus helped had been dealing with an issue for TWELVE years. The same amount of time Jairus had been watching his dream grow up, this other woman had a dream of being healed from an issue of blood that had plagued her everyday. One dream that was twelve years old was about to die while another dream that was twelve years old was about to live! When God is not answering your prayer, He is answering someone's prayer somewhere else!

If your dream looks dead, there is somebody, somewhere, whose dream just came back to life.

As a Christian, we should be able to rejoice in knowing that God is working somewhere even if it does not look like He is working in our situation. Our present situation or circumstance is never a deciding factor on who God is. It is so immature for a Christian to lose trust in God just because our life may be in a temporary place of struggle.

- Just because you have not got healed does not mean that somebody else is not getting healed
- Just because your son has not got saved does not mean that somebody's son just didn't get saved.
- Just because your hopes are dying does not mean that God isn't bringing hope somewhere else

My point is that God is who He says He is. God will do what He says He will do, but it will be in His time.

We do not know what Jairus was thinking because the Bible does not tell us, but I wonder what he thought when news arrived that his little girl was dead. He probably thought that Jesus was too late. He probably thought that Jesus had missed it.

It is funny because the Bible tells us that someone told him to quit bothering Jesus because his girl was already dead. I have found in life that there is always somebody to tell you to give up on Jesus. There is always somebody to tell you that it is too late. There is always somebody to tell you that your dream is dead and nothing can change it now.

It is easy to quit when things do not look good. It is easy to quit when your hopes are dying. But let me tell you this, it is not easy to quit when you really got it. In fact, I believe that it is impossible to quit once you really got it. I don't think Jesus can be washed off. I don't think Jesus is like a temporary tattoo-here today and gone tomorrow. I don't think Jesus is like your summer friend-hang out with him but when school starts back you don't know him. I don't think Jesus is a contact lens that can give you sight one day but be in the trash the next. I don't think Jesus is like the paper plate-use Him to get full then crumble Him up. I don't think Jesus is like the last pick on the playground-let Him be on your team until something better comes along. Maybe you are talking about a different Jesus. Maybe you are talking about an imposter Jesus. Maybe you are talking about an imitation Jesus because the Jesus I know you couldn't walk away from Him because the Bible says He orders my steps. The Jesus I know you couldn't turn your back on Him because He's got my back. The Jesus I know you couldn't sell Him out because I already sold Him out and He still went to the cross for me!

The Jesus I know loves me and is patient with me and cares so deeply for me that I could never really quit on Him because I would have nowhere else to go. When is it time to stop trusting Him? How about when your dream dies? Listen carefully, you can trust Him even when your dream is dead.

This little girl was dead and He was still in control. Think about it, you can trust Him even when your dream dies. God may not totally resurrect your dead dreams, but I promise you this, you can trust Him even when they are dead. Jesus stepped in the home of Jairus and brought life back to this little girl's body; He raised the dead. He can bring dead dreams back to life. I long for the day when church is full of people who truly trust God with dead dreams.

You see, when Jesus is the center of all your hopes and dreams your dreams can never really die because Jesus already came back from the dead. Let Jesus be your hope today. If you have some dead dreams today will you still place your trust in God concerning whatever it is? The good news for us is that we can still trust God even when all our hope dies.

Chapter 8

SHAKE IT OFF WHERE IT CAME FROM

The Apostle Paul and many other men were on a ship when a storm came up and tore the ship into pieces. God already came to Paul and told him that there would be a shipwreck and that no one would lose their life. Sometimes God will rescue you in the storm, but sometimes He just preserves you through the storm. Just because you made it through the storm in one piece does not mean that the trial is over. Sometimes it is after the storm that the old serpent will rise up and strike at you with all his energy.

It is not always sunny skies after the storm; sometimes the rain continues. Your dream may go through many rainy days, but God is always the light behind the clouds. What do we do after making it through the storm only to find that we have been snake bit again? The answer is we shake if off where it came from.

Sometimes God will rescue you in the storm, but sometimes He just preserves you through the storm.

Paul had the opportunity to shake if off where it came from. It was after surviving the stormy seas that Paul was faced with another obstacle. Before one trial could end, another one already fastened itself to his hand. He responded by shaking it off where it came from.

"And when they had been brought safely through, then we found out that the island was called Malta. And the natives showed us extraordinary kindness; for because of the rain that had set in and because of the cold, they kindled a fire and received us all. But when Paul had gathered a bundle of sticks and laid them on the fire, a viper came out because of the heat, and fastened on his hand. And when the natives saw the creature hanging from his hand, they began saying to one another, 'undoubtedly this man is a murderer, and though he had been saved from the sea, justice has not allowed him to live.' However he shook the creature

off into the fire and suffered no harm." Acts
28:1-5

The Bible tells us that Paul landed on the Island of
Malta. Malta was not his homeland. Malta was not a
place of security for Paul. I believe in many ways Malta
represented the world's answer after the storm. This
world is not our place of shelter; this world is not our
answer after the storm. The Bible says in verse two that
the natives showed much kindness to him. I want you
to understand that the world will try to buddy up to
you as long as they don't know that you are buddies
with Jesus.

I want to be buddies with Jesus! I like the old song
that says just give me Jesus.

Verse two says some other interesting things about
Malta. We are told that Malta was a cloudy place. You
might be thinking that you don't remember that. Well,
the Bible said that it was raining, and you can't have rain
without clouds. Malta was a cloudy place. It is like the
world we live in today; we live in a cloudy world. People
are cloudy concerning their purpose. People are cloudy
concerning the truth. People are cloudy concerning
what is right and wrong. We live in a cloudy place.

Malta was not only a cloudy place, but it was also
a cold place. The Bible made a point to mention that it
was cold. You know the Bible says that as the clouds of

the end of the age begin to assemble that the colder the earth is going to be.

> *"And because lawlessness is increased, most people's love will grow cold."* Matthew 24:12

One of the signs of the end of the age is that sin will increase and that the world will become a colder place to live (spiritually speaking).

Sin seems to be increasing in every area of life. There is sin in the White House. Today we pass laws to make people think what God has called wrong is somehow right. We murder babies every year in the name of fairness and make a law to say it is ok. We legalize things like alcohol and drugs and say it is up to each individual.

There is not only sin in the White House but there is sin in the Court House. We give people rights they shouldn't have and by doing so we facilitate their wrong doing. If you go into jail today with a masters degree on crime you will come out with a doctorate degree on crime because we facilitate wrong doing.

There is sin in the White House, the Court House, and sin in the School House. You can pass out a condom in school, but a Gideon cannot go and pass out a Bible. You can talk about anything and everything in schools but Jesus.

There is sin in the White House, the Court House, the School House, and sin the Church House. Preachers today have forgotten what true preaching really is. Churches today focus more on worldly things than the things of God. We need to forget about religion and get serious about Jesus! There must be a change in our churches.

There is sin the White House, the Court House, the School House, the Church House, and nothing will change until you get the sin out of Your House. The Bible tells us to get our own house in order. Most parents let their kids do stuff that their parents would have never dreamed of. The home has become a den of devils instead of the place ordained by God for safety and encouragement. The home has been wronged by violence, divorce, child abuse, and incest. We need for God to bring healing to the homes of America. Sin in our own house will cause us to be cold toward the things of God. It will harden your heart toward the church. It will harden your heart toward His plan and purpose for your life. Don't let your home be a cold place.

Malta was a cloudy place and a cold place, but it was one more thing-it was a cursed place. The Bible says that they tried to build a fire to stay warm. People have been trying to build fires to keep themselves warm for centuries...figuratively speaking. Some think that money will keep them warm on the inside. Some think that pleasure will keep them warm on the inside. Some think that recognition or attention will warm them up, but I am telling you that outside of Jesus Christ and having a relationship with Him there is nothing that can keep you warm on the inside.

They tried to build a fire but it did not do the trick. What we build will bite us, but what God builds will bless us. Inside the fire was a snake. The snake has forever been a symbol of being cursed from when God cursed the devil back in the Garden of Eden. Get the picture, this snake jumps out at Paul and it represents the fact that the enemy is always trying to send a curse our way. The enemy is always trying to bite the man or woman of God.

The good news is that my Bible says that through Jesus we can reject any form of curse that is put upon us. Galatians 3:13-14 *"Christ redeemed us from the curse of the Law, having become a curse for us…in order that in Christ Jesus the blessing of Abraham might come to the Gentiles, so that we might receive the promise of the Spirit through faith."*

Isn't that great? We are not cursed but blessed. The Apostle Paul knew that. When the time came that the devil tried to curse him he just shook it off. In fact, he shook it off where it came from. It came from the fire and it needs to go back to the fire!

What is interesting is that it wasn't until Paul threw some sticks on that fire that the snake jumped out at him. The Bible says there was a mediocre, dim, weak, flickering fire. I just believe Paul got tired of watching that sorry excuse for a fire and decided he was going to do something to get that thing going. Let me tell you something, when the man or woman of God decide they are going to do something to get a real fire going for the glory of God is when the devil will strike out.

The people of God have watched a weak excuse for the church long enough. It is time we get a real fire going for His glory that will burn revival all over this country! But rest assured, when you decide to stir up the devil's comfortable, cozy resting place, he will be ready to strike at you at your most powerful point.

Did you notice that the snake jumped out at Paul's hand. Do you know why? Because a few verses later Paul used that hand to heal somebody. In many ways, that hand was a central point of Paul's ministry. Often, that is how the devil will try to attack. He will come at you at your most central point of ministry. The devil wants to poison the central part of the ministry God has given you. Don't let the devil get you swelled up. If he swells you up you will not be effective for the glory of God. Just shake it off. Next time the old serpent comes at you, just shake him off where he came from. Next time he tempts you to sin just shake him off to the fire. Next time he tries to bring you down just shake him off to the fire. Next time he attacks your marriage just shake him off to the fire. Next time he comes at your dream just shake him off to the fire.

The devil will try to poison the dream that God has given to you but you need to remember to shake him off to the fire.

Chapter 9

Conflicting Expectations

Everyday we wake up with certain expectations for what our life will be like; everybody expects something. Maybe you have not given much thought to the subject, but everybody has expectations for their life, their job, their children, their marriage...etc. Expectations are apart of our everyday lives. An expectation is a belief that is centered on your future.

Did you know that Heaven has expectations for you?

God has something out there in your future that He wants you to achieve. In fact, God has an expectation for you. He expects you to fulfill a certain number of things.

Did you know that Hell has expectations for you?

The devil and his demons are trying to mess with your future. In fact, our enemy has an expectation for you. He expects you to respond negatively in certain avenues of your life. He expects you to fall and give up everything you have worked for. You see, in our world today there are conflicting expectations.

I want you to think back to last chapter. We read about how the Apostle Paul was bitten by a poisonous snake. A snake came out from a bundle of sticks and bit Paul on his right hand. After the snake bite, the Bible says something very interesting.

> *"But they were EXPECTING that he was about to swell up or suddenly fall down dead."* Acts 28:6

Did you catch that? We are told that the people EXPECTED Paul to swell up or drop dead. I began to think about that and it hit me that the devil expects us to respond a certain way when he attacks us. Think about it. This snake bit Paul and induced him with venom that <u>should have</u> made him sick. I said should have. God's people have a lot of should haves. Should have died, but I didn't. Should have got sick, but I didn't. Should have been in a wreck, but I wasn't. You see, the hand of God can change the should haves.

Paul should have swelled up, gotten weak, and possibly died. That is what the enemy expected. I am telling you today that Hell has some expectations for your life.

The devil expects you to give up on your dream. The demons expect you to forfeit everything you have worked for. The enemy expects you to give up on your marriage. Hell has some expectations for you!

The devil expects you to curse God when you get that report. The devil expects you to give up when your kids get into trouble. The devil expects you to fall into sin every time a temptation comes your way. He expects you to quit church every time someone makes you mad. He expects you to get bitter when someone hurts you. The world expects you to give up on Christianity. They say, 'he will be back doing the same thing he was doing in a couple of months.' They say, 'just give her a few more weeks and she will be back into it again.'

As a Senior in high school, my friends expected me to be back into the drug scene. My girlfriend expected me to act the same way I use to. A decade later and praise God I am still preaching! A decade later and praise God I am still fighting the devil for every inch! A decade later and praise God I am still living it!

I know that they were not expecting it, but I have different expectations.

- I am expecting to grow closer with God as the days go by.
- I am expecting to see His hand work.
- I am expecting to see miracles happen as I walk this path.
- I am expecting deliverance from any sin that haunts me.
- I am expecting God's dream for my life to become a reality.

You see, the hand of God can change the should haves

Do not let Hell unload its expectations on you. You need to get full of the expectations that Heaven has for you. Don't expect the worse, expect the best. Don't expect curses, expect blessings. Don't expect fear, expect faith. Don't expect death, expect deliverance. Don't expect bondage, expect breakthrough. Don't expect shame, expect the Savior.

There are conflicting expectations today. Don't get swelled up or lose heart or drop dead. Instead, expect that God will be God in your life. The reason that Paul did not react to that snake bite is because he had a different set of expectations.

"According to my earnest EXPECTATION and hope, that I shall not be put to shame

in anything, but that with all boldness,
Christ shall even now, as always, be exalted
in my body, whether by life or by death."
Philippians 1:20

Do you know why Paul had so much confidence in his future? The reason is because he already met his future on the Damascus road. When Paul met Jesus Christ, his future was forever different.

One of my favorite movies of all time is the 1980's flick "Back to the Future." I have always been interested in the idea of time travel…but anyway…let me tell you something…you don't have to get into an 80's model DeLorian and get it up to 88 miles an hour to travel into your future. The moment you got saved you met your future! Your future is wrapped up in a person.

Just like Paul, we can be confident in our future because we have met our future. Our future is more than a place or more than possessions; our future is a person. We need to begin everyday believing and expecting to see that hand of God at work. We need to expect God to carry out the dream that He has put in our heart. We need to expect what the Bible says we should expect.

> *"From henceforth EXPECTING till his*
> *enemies be made his footstool." (KJV)*
> Hebrews 10:13

It is time for Christians to start expecting that our enemies can be our footstool. So many Christians are afraid of their past and afraid of falling back into sin... you need to be expecting holiness and sanctification instead. You need to be expecting victory at your doorpost.

> *"For I know the thoughts that I think toward*
> *you, saith the Lord, thoughts of peace, and*
> *not of evil, to give you an EXPECTED*
> *end." (KJV)* Jeremiah 29:11

God said that He wanted to give you and expected end. What are you expecting today?

For many people, they are expecting to get sick. For many people they are expecting to lose their retirement money. For many people they are expecting to die in bad health. For what you expect in your heart is what you are going to get.

> *"For as he thinketh in his heart, so is he."*
> *(KJV)* Proverbs 23:7

You know the old saying 'you are what you eat?' If that were true we would be in trouble for sure. The truth is, you are what you think. You are what you expect. The world we live in has conflicting expectations for you today. The only way your dream will become a reality is to expect what the Bible says you need to expect.

Chapter 10

Building The Wall While Battling The Enemy

One woman thought she was doing pretty good when she went to the doctor. On her papers she put down that she weighed 150 pounds. When they actually weighed her, the scales said she weighed 210 pounds. On her papers she put down that she was 5'8. When they actually measured her, they found out that she was 5 foot even. When they took her blood pressure they found that it was unusually high. The doctor asked her about this to which the lady responded by saying 'well, I came in here thinking I was 5'8 and 150 only to find out that I was 5'0 and 210. What did you expect my blood pressure to do!'

If we are not careful, it will not take much to disappoint us. Sometimes we have unreal expectations and the result can be devastating; sometimes the truth is ugly. Many believers have unreal expectations for their dream. There is no such thing as a "perfect marriage." There is no such thing as a "perfect job." There is no such thing a "perfect church." Not everybody will support you. Not everybody will like you. Not everybody will work for you.

One thing is for sure today and you need to understand it-the devil will have something on assignment to keep your dream from happening. Nothing great takes place without some form of resistance. It is an unreal expectation to think that your dream will be easy to accomplish. The ugly truth is that while you are building the wall you will also be battling the enemy.

This is illustrated for us in the Bible. One of the most inspiring books in all the Bible is the book of Nehemiah. God gave the task to Nehemiah to rebuild the city of Jerusalem because it had been torn down. They worked endlessly to fulfill the call that God had given them. In the midst of the people following God and being obedient to the Lord, their was a group of people who rose up and tried to come against the leadership of Nehemiah.

It is interesting because the Bible tells us that there was a "secret meeting" that took place to conspire against Nehemiah. I am convinced that anytime the devil wants to come against the things of God there is always a secret meeting. Many marriages have been destroyed because of secret meetings between two individuals. Many churches have been destroyed because of secret meetings between groups in the church (the preacher in me wants to start preaching right now but I will move on).

The thing that you need to understand today is that there is really no such thing as a secret meeting because God knows everything. Praise God! You do not need to fear because God knows how the enemy is trying to come against your dream. You do not need to fret because God knows the strategy that is out against you.

Nehemiah had a dream to see the walls of Jerusalem be built back up, and he believed God would carry him through it till the end. Think about it for a minute. God loves to take something that has been broken down so that He can build it back up. God is good at putting the pieces back together.

- Is your life broken down today? I know someone who can put it back together.
- Is your marriage broken down today? I know someone who can put it back together.
- Is your emotions broken down today? I know someone who can put it back together.

We serve a God that specializes in taking what is broken and putting it back together. Nehemiah had a dream to see the walls built back up, but it was not going to be easy. He knew that he would be building the wall while battling the enemy.

What is the wall that must be built to see your dream accomplished?

Understand now that through the entire process you will be building the wall while battling the enemy. I think most of the time a person will give up the first time resistance starts. Pastor, if you give up the first time resistance starts, then you will never stay at a church more than about a year or two. Business man, if you give up the first time resistance starts, then you will never see your project get off the ground. School teacher, if you give up the first time resistance starts, then you will never deposit anything valuable into the life of your student.

Never give up. Instead, look up. Look up toward Heaven and give it all to God through prayer. When the enemy tries to raise up its head it is time for the child of God to bow his. Prayer goes a long way. Praying will get you in trouble and praying will get you out of trouble. Praying will get you in trouble with the devil. I don't know about you but I am not trying to make friends with the devil. Sometimes praying will get you in trouble. It was praying that caused Daniel to get in trouble, but it was also praying that shut the mouth of that lion too! It was praying that put those three Hebrew boys in a furnace, but it was praying that kept them from burning too! The only way your dream can became a reality is to bathe it in prayer.

Nehemiah bathed his dream in prayer. He knew that fulfilling God's task was not going to be easy. Nehemiah knew that he must continue to build the wall while battling the enemy.

One of my favorite verses in all the Bible is Nehemiah 4:17. The Bible says *"those who were rebuilding the wall and those who carried burdens took their load with one hand doing the work and the other holding a weapon."*

Think about it. The Bible says they had a brick in one hand and a sword in the other. I love that! They couldn't come down from the wall because it was necessary to continue doing what God called them to do. So instead of coming down, they worked with one hand and fought with the other. Hallelujah! Maybe it is the "Gladiator"spirit that is in most guys, I don't know, but something about that makes me want to jump up there on that wall and help them.

One truth we can definitely see from this passage is that there is always a fight before a victory. Moses had to confront Pharaoh before the people could follow him out. Joshua had to go through Jericho before he could take the land. David had a giant in his path before becoming king. Jesus had a cross before He could rise on the third day.

Serving God is a brick in one hand and a sword in the other. I am not suggesting that we need to go back to the days of the Crusades, but I am suggesting that we need to understand that our dream will not come without a fight.

Chapter 11

Never Allow Your Memories To Be Greater Than Your Dreams

"Where there is no vision, the people are unrestrained." Proverbs 29:18

If a person quits dreaming, they will cast off restraint in areas of their life and the result will be detrimental. So often, people allow their memories to be greater than their dreams. Memories are not all that bad. I have some great memories from childhood of going to sporting events with my dad. I have some great memories of gathering over at my grandparents' house on Christmas Eve. I have some great memories with friends on vacation or some special occasion. Memories are not all that bad.

I hope that as you read this book you can think of some good memories you have shared with the people you love. Not all memories are good memories though. You may remember something that causes you great pain. You may remember something that deeply troubles you. You may remember something that haunts you everyday. Memories can brighten our day or cause us to be depressed…it depends on the memory.

Whatever the case, never allow your memories to be greater than your dreams. For many people, they spend all their time thinking about past events. Many think about missed opportunities or how they messed up. Many think about great achievements or some monumental victory. Whether it is something good or something bad, we should not spend all our time thinking about the past.

Thinking too much about failures or too much about victories can keep us from accomplishing what we need to accomplish today. As you study the Bible you will find out that God places much emphasis on today. Throughout scripture, God makes a point to show the importance of today.

> *"Give us THIS DAY our daily bread."*
> Matthew 6:11

> *"He again fixes a certain day, TODAY, saying through David after so long a time just as has been said before, TODAY if you*

hear His voice, do not harden your hearts."
Hebrews 4:7

The reason today is so important is because today may be the only day we have. Yesterday is gone and tomorrow may never come. We need to spend each day living out our dream the best that we know how. Never allow your memories to be greater than your dreams! I still believe the best in yet to come! I still believe my best days and your best days are ahead. I always tell our church that our best days are ahead. I really believe that.

It saddens me in church because so many talk about God like He is the "God of yesterday." Almost as if He cannot do the things today that we read about in the Bible. God is the God of yesterday, but He is also the God of today and tomorrow! My memories of God are great, but I am expecting to see greater things every day that I follow Him. I do not believe Satan's lie that God does not move today like He did in the past. I do not believe Satan's lie that God does not do the miraculous or that God is somehow different. My Bible says that *"Jesus Christ is the same yesterday and today and forever."* Hebrews 13:8 That is simple enough for me.

I believe we live in a day where God wants to do **greater** things now on the earth than ever before. I believe we live in a day where God wants to do **greater** miracles now than has ever been seen. Listen what Isaiah the prophet said.

> *"Do not call to mind the former things, or ponder things of the past. Behold, I will do something new, now it will spring forth; will you not be aware of it? I will even make a roadway in the wilderness, rivers in the desert."* Isaiah 43:18-19

The book of Ecclesiastes speaks to this as well.

> *"Do not say, why is it that the former days were better than these?"* Ecclesiastes 3:10

We need to be careful as a church culture not to get the mindset thinking it "was better yesterday than now." So many people talk about "the good ole days." How good where they? In our own country we say the same thing, but when you think about it, the past had some awful moments too.

Think about the 1920's and 1930's. People will remember those decades as some of the most colorful in American history. Think about the birth of Jazz music, and for the first time movies were beginning to have some color. Some good memories are from the 20's and 30's, but do you remember the Great Depression? It was during those times that the world went through one of the hardest eras.

People will talk about the 40's and how great it was to be alive then. Those were the days when you didn't have to lock your door at night. That does sound great compared to today, but the 40's also had some tragic events as well. World War II took place during that decade. Thank God if you served in that war. My grandfather served and I have respect for every person in the military, but WWII was a world-wide event that many lost their life in.

People will remember the 50's and think about the malt shops and poodle skirts. Everyone remembers the music from the 50's and how it changed music forever. Good times, right? The 50's also brought about the rise of Communism.

Who can forget the 60's? The 60's are treasured in American history because of hit TV shows and the boom of technology. Do you know what else happened in the 60's? The 60's saw Martin Luther King Jr. and John F. Kennedy assassinated.

What about the 70's? The 70's were the time of free love and peace. With free love and peace came disease and loss. The 80's saw the Cold War escalate and the AIDS epidemic. The 90's witnessed the Gulf War and presidential failures. In 2001, we witnessed the World Trade Center tragedy. My point is that every generation has seen some tragic events. My point is that "the good ole days" had some not so good moments.

If we are not careful, we will begin to think that our best days are behind us. The truth of the matter is, the best is yet to come. Never allow your memories to be greater than your dreams.

Many in the church believe that as the time approaches for Christ to return, the Church is going to get worse and worse. Although I do believe the "false church" will get worse and worse, I believe the true saints of God will become more pure and more holy as the time approaches. It is like a bride before a wedding. As the day approaches, she is making herself more ready. We are the bride of Christ, and I am convinced that God is making us ready for the moment that Jesus takes His bride! The world will get worse and worse and the true church will get cleaner and cleaner. Our best days are yet to come.

Eventually, we will be in perfect peace with God for all eternity. Our best days are yet to come! We should never have a frown on our face because of that truth. Let us live each day with the realization that Jesus is coming back; that is a fact. Our best days are yet to come.

Chapter 12

THE TASSEL IS WORTH THE HASSLE

When a high school student graduates high school it is a very important event in their life because they have been promoted to a new stage in life. Life is filled with promotions. When most people think about a promotion they only think about a raise in money or a new job, but in reality, a promotion is to advance in growth and prosperity.

Life is filled with opportunities for all of us to be promoted. In our relationship with God, He desires that we pass the tests that He places in front of us so that He can promote us to new stages in life. You may be reading this book and God is still waiting for you to pass your exit exam to go to the next grade. You should be in advanced Calculus by now, but you are still struggling with your multiplication tables.

Multiplication tables are for 3rd graders. It is sad, but there are so many in the church that are still in the elementary school of Christianity. They have not passed the tests and so they have not been promoted by God to a new place. God wants you to wear a spiritual tassel on your cap because He wants to graduate you in life.

In the first chapter of this book I made a reference to Joseph. *"Then Joseph had a dream, and when he told it to his brothers, they hated him even more."* <u>Genesis 37:5</u>

Young Joseph was a dreamer. Joseph had a dream that he would be a great leader. His story is one of the most interesting in the Bible. God promoted Joseph from living in an Egyptian dungeon to ruling the nation and spending his nights in the palace. The story of Joseph is one of my favorites in all the Bible. You know his story. His father loved him very much, and he gave him a multicolored coat that made his brothers very angry. Out of jealousy, his brothers threw him into a pit and faked his death. They eventually sold him as a slave to a caravan of travelers headed to Egypt.

Joseph was 17 years old when these events took place in his life...the same age as some high school graduates...the same age I was when God called me to preach. It is hard to even imagine being alone in Egypt serving as a slave in someone else's home. It would have been easy for Joseph to give up on God. It would have been easy for Joseph to become bitter and hateful; that is not what he did. Joseph knew that God was in control and that all the events of his life would turn out for the glory of God. He knew that these things were testing his faith and that God was going to promote him when the time was right. Joseph knew that the tassel would be worth the hassle.

The final chapter of this book is entitled the tassel is worth the hassle because when God does promote you to fulfill your dream, it will be worth it. Three simple points I want you to remember concerning the story of Joseph are to never give in, never give up, and never give out.

First of all, never give in. If you know the story of Joseph, you know that he resisted temptation. The Bible teaches us that one day a beautiful woman made a pass at him...and he literally ran the opposite direction; he resisted temptation. Temptation will come at you everyday in some form for the rest of your life. Someone once said "why does opportunity only knock once, but temptation knocks everyday." I think there is a lot of truth to that.

When the devil opens a door, don't even take time to shut it-just run the other direction.

When the devil opens a door, don't even take time to think about it-just run the other direction.

When the devil opens a door, don't even take time to weigh out the options-just run the other direction.

YOU NEED TO MAKE UP YOUR MIND NOW THAT YOU ARE NOT GOING TO GIVE IN.

Temptation will come at your dream in some way or another. Resists the devil and he will flee from you. Joseph was a man who pursued God and left everything else behind. He was a graduate in God's school because he would never give in.

Not only did he have the attitude of never giving in, but also, he had the attitude to never give up. There will be days in your life when you feel like giving up. If the devil can get you to give up, he knows he will win. He wants you to give up on your family. He wants you to give up on your marriage. He wants you to give up on your dreams. Hold on until the end. Don't let go of what God has shown you!

IT IS ALWAYS TOO SOON TO QUIT

God can resurrect anything in your life. They said after Lazarus died that it was too late. It had been four days, but God brought him back to life again. Some have said in your own life that it is too late, but God showed them. He brought you back to life! Some have said your church is dead, but God can bring it back to life. God can resurrect anything. It is always too soon to quit because we serve a God that can bring things back to life.

2,000 years ago, Jesus Christ hung on a cross and went to a tomb and the Roman soldiers and the devil and all the demons were happy…but God brought Him back to life. Those disciples had given up too soon. They watched as all their hopes died. They watched as all their futures died. They watched as all their expectations died. THEY GAVE UP. Praise God! Those boys got to see all their dreams rise again.

So often, we think our dreams are dying right in front of us, when in reality, they are just being born. Don't ever mistake birth pains for death pains. Just ask any woman that has ever given birth and I am sure they will tell you that they felt like they were about to die! Do you know why? It hurts to give birth.

You may look at your situation and mistake death pains for birth pains. God has not given up on you. He wants to birth new things in your life. After being promoted, God birthed new things in the life of Joseph; Joseph had two sons. The names of these two boys are very significant because they speak to Joseph's situation. We should always speak to our situation and never let our situation speak to us.

He named his first son "Manasseh." What a great name. The reason this name is so great is because the meaning it carries with it. The name Manasseh means that God has made me to forget all my troubles.

It would not be a bad idea for us to birth a Manasseh in our own life. God can cause you to forget the things that haunt you. God can cause you to forget the bad things that have happened to you. Some of you will never fulfill your dream until you forget all your troubles. God can help you to forget.

Joseph named his other son "Ephraim." This name is also significant. Ephraim means that God has made me fruitful in the land of my affliction. Isn't that good? God can bless you even in a desolate place.

Promotion brings across the idea of birthing new things in your life. Remember, don't mistake birth pains for death pains. As God births your dream there will be some hurt. There will be days of hardship. Always remember that it is always too soon to quit. Whatever you do, never give up.

Joseph knew to never give in, never give up, and never give out. Joseph knew to never give out revenge. Never give out what people deserve. Joseph could have tried to take revenge on all the people that had hurt him, but he had a different perspective on his situation.

> *"And as for you, you meant evil against me, but God meant it for good in order to bring about this present result, to preserve many people alive."* Genesis 50:20

In essence, Joseph said that what man meant for bad God meant for good. What you need to realize today is that sometimes when people try to hurt you, they are actually helping you get to the place that God has for you. God will even use evil people to push you into a place of blessing.

Don't ever try to take revenge into your own hands because you don't know how God is going to use the circumstances in your life. Joseph made up his mind that he was not going to give out what people deserved. He had the chance to get all the revenge he wanted on his brothers, but he did not pursue the opportunity. Instead of giving out revenge, he invited them up to his table to share a meal.

Let God promote you to a new place by passing the tests that He places in front of you. The dream that God has put into your heart can become a reality if you will trust God completely. The tassel will be worth the hassle.